The Biggest Thrill Rides

Susan K. Mitchell
AR B.L.: 5.7
Points: 1.0   MG

MEGASTRUCTURES

THE BIGGEST THRILL RIDES

by Susan K. Mitchell

Gareth Stevens
Publishing

Please visit our web site at: www.garethstevens.com
For a free color catalog describing Gareth Stevens Publishing's
list of high-quality books, call 1-800-542-2595 (USA)
or 1-800-387-3178 (Canada).

Library of Congress Cataloging-in-Publication Data

Mitchell, Susan K.
  The biggest thrill rides / by Susan K. Mitchell.
    p. cm. — (Megastructures)
  Includes bibliographical references and index.
  ISBN-10: 0-8368-8361-6 (lib. btg.)
  ISBN-13: 978-0-8368-8361-9 (lib. bdg.)
  1. Roller coasters. 2. Amusement rides. I. Title.
 GV1860.R64M58   2007
 791.06'8—dc22   2007006197

This edition first published in 2008 by
Gareth Stevens Publishing
A Weekly Reader® Company
1 Reader's Digest Road
Pleasantville, NY 10570-7000 USA

Editorial direction: Mark J. Sachner
Editor: Barbara Kiely Miller
Art direction and design: Tammy West
Picture research: Diane Laska-Swanke
Production: Jessica Yanke
Illustrations: Spectrum Creative Inc.

Picture credits: Cover, title, pp. 6, 7, 9, 17, 22, 29 © Coasterimage.com;
p. 5 © Hulton Archive/Getty Images; p. 14 © Kelly-Mooney Photography/
CORBIS; pp. 16, 19, 20, 24, 26 © AP Images; p. 27 © Noah K. Murray/
Star Ledger/CORBIS

Printed in the United States of America

1 2 3 4 5 6 7 8 9 11 10 09 08 07

CONTENTS

On the Cover: The Top Thrill Dragster in Sandusky, Ohio, was the very first full-circuit roller coaster to top the 400-foot- (122-meter-) high mark.

THE EARLIEST COASTERS

Anyone who has been to an amusement park has heard it — screams followed by the whoosh of racing coaster cars on steel tracks. Thrill seekers come from all over for a rush they can only get from a roller coaster. Not many people will ever take off in an F-18 fighter jet. Few will cliff dive from 400 feet (122 meters). Even fewer will sit in the cockpit of the Space Shuttle and blast into space. Most of us can come close to experiencing all these thrills, however, on an extreme roller coaster.

Roller coasters and other thrill rides have come a long way since the 1600s. The first thrill rides were ice slides. Russians built simple wooden ramps covered with ice. Winters are extremely cold in Russia, so the ice could become very thick. The ramps were just wide enough for a small sled. People climbed a 70-foot (21-m) ladder and sat on the sled. With one push, riders slipped and slid down the huge icy ramp.

Like a Runaway Train!
Ice slides are great in the winter. The only problem is that without ice there can be no ice slides. During the 1700s, Russian ruler Catherine the Great wanted the thrill of an ice slide available all year. She had

This **1825** drawing is titled "The Flying Mountain." It shows what a nineteenth century wooden ice slide looked like.

workers build a sled with wheels. With this new sled, she could enjoy summer sliding as well.

In the 1800s, France borrowed the idea of ice slides. Since winters in France are not as cold or icy as those in Russia, however, the French had to make a few changes. The French people needed a way to slide down a dry ramp. To help move their sled along, they put wooden rollers on the ramp. This addition inspired the name "roller coaster."

The first thrill ride in the United States was built in Pennsylvania in the late 1800s. The Mauch Chunk Switchback Railway was an old coal mining route. The railway wound its way up and around a

MEGA FACTS

The first roller coaster with a steel track was the Matterhorn Bobsled. The ride opened in 1959 at Disneyland in Anaheim, California.

Coney Island

The grandfather of amusement parks in the United States is Coney Island Park. In 1895, Paul Boyton opened Sea Lion Park at Coney Island, near New York City. It was the first real amusement park in the United States. Inspired by this park, in 1897, George Tilyou opened Steeplechase Park at Coney Island.

People paid twenty-five cents to get inside Steeplechase Park. In every direction, people found flashing lights, noisy games, and amazing rides. Through the early 1900s, other amusement parks began to spring up at Coney Island. All of the original parks have since been torn down. One of the amazing rides that survived, however, is the Cyclone.

First opened in 1927, the Cyclone still runs today. It is considered one of the world's most exciting roller coasters. It has been operated by Astroland Park since 1975. The Cyclone is a 2,640-foot- (805-m-) long wooden roller coaster. It is 85 feet (26 m) high and can reach a top speed of 60 miles (97 kilometers) per hour.

mountain. After the coal mine went out of business, the railway was opened to sightseers in 1873. For the price of one dollar, people could ride up the mountain. The railroad cars were hauled uphill by a steam engine. After it reached the top, the train coasted back down the mountain.

True roller coasters did not show up until a few years later. LaMarcus A. Thompson had ridden the Mauch Chunk Switchback in Pennsylvania. He got an idea to build a ride like it. Thompson designed the Switchback Railway.

In 1991, the Cyclone was named a New York City historic landmark.

The ride opened in 1884 at Coney Island near Brooklyn, New York. It was a huge hit!

Riders paid five cents to climb up to a 50-foot- (15-m-) high platform. They sat in an open, sledlike car. The car rumbled up and down several small hills at only 6 miles (10 km) per hour, which is little more than a crawl by today's standards. Riders back then loved the Switchback Railway, however, and the roller coaster craze was born.

Throughout the 1900s, roller coasters kept getting bigger, faster, and taller. Designers figured out how to add loops and twists. Amusement and theme parks came up with new ideas for rides. The thrill rides just kept coming. These early roller coasters, however, would be nothing compared to the extreme thrill rides of today.

The bright blue Millennium Force coaster in Sandusky, Ohio, has high hills, two tunnels, and overbanked turns (*below*).

TOO DANGEROUS?

In 1997, the Roller Coaster Corporation of America came up with an amazing idea. They wanted to build the world's first looping wooden roller coaster. They talked to officials at Paramount King's Island, an amusement park in Cincinnati, Ohio, about building it there.

Two years later, builders began construction on the Son of Beast — which would be the name of the coaster. Workers dug deep holes in the ground for the support footings. They filled the holes with steel-reinforced concrete. These footings would support the weight of the coaster framework, its track, the trains, and the passengers who ride in them.

Wooden boards were shipped to the coaster's building site. Son of Beast used more than 300 miles (483 km) of timber in its construction. Workers bolted the wood together to form large sections of the track. Giant cranes lifted each section onto the framework so it could be bolted into place.

The wooden track was built in several layers. The top layers of any wooden roller coaster track are wider than the bottom layers. The layers create an overhang, or groove, on the inside of the tracks for the safety wheels of the roller coaster car. These

Besides having exciting spiral turns (*above*), the Son of Beast holds the record for the largest drop at 214 feet (65 m).

safety wheels keep the cars from flying off the tracks. The only way to remove the roller coaster cars is by unbolting the track itself.

Loop de Loop

Then it was time to build the loop. Since wood cannot be bent into a loop shape, steel was also used on Son of Beast. Designers created the

MEGA FACTS

Son of Beast is considered a terrain roller coaster because it rises and falls like the land around it.

May the Force(s) Be With You

Roller coasters use many different forces to move train cars along the tracks. Special motors pull the train cars to the top of the first hill. Some trains are pulled by a chain that runs between the track and hooks onto the cars. Once the cars reach the dizzying height of the first hill, gravity takes over and pulls the train down the hill fast. As the train races down the hill, it picks up speed. This increase in speed forces the train up smaller hills and around sharp bends — even through twists and loops — without any more help from motors.

When the ride comes to an end, the train car wheels rub against the roller coaster track, producing friction. This force slows the momentum of the train. Momentum is the force that keeps an object moving until it comes to a complete stop. Special brakes help increase the friction until the train comes to a safe stop back at the loading station.

118-foot- (36-m-) high loop using a steel frame. Then they covered the wooden track with steel.

Son of Beast opened to the public on May 26, 2000. When it opened, it shattered almost every record held by a wooden roller coaster. It is the tallest wooden coaster in the world at 218 feet (66 m) high. At a top speed of 78 miles (126 km) per hour, Son of Beast is also

Three different sets of wheels work together to help keep coaster cars on the tracks and riders safe. The green bars show the points of contact between the wheels and the track.

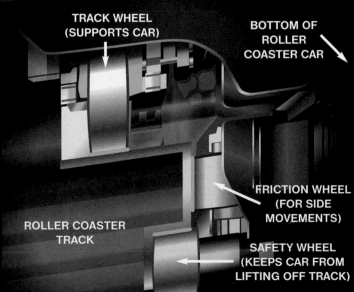

ROLLER COASTER

TRACK WHEEL
(SUPPORTS CAR)

BOTTOM OF
ROLLER
COASTER CAR

FRICTION WHEEL
(FOR SIDE
MOVEMENTS)

ROLLER COASTER
TRACK

SAFETY WHEEL
(KEEPS CAR FROM
LIFTING OFF TRACK)

faster than any other wooden roller coaster in the world.

Since opening, however, Son of Beast has had a few problems. Some riders have complained of injuries while riding the coaster. On July 9, 2006, more than twenty people were hurt. The riders received injuries to the head or neck. None of the injuries received were life threatening, but several people had to stay in the hospital.

Paramount King's Island officials closed Son of Beast. They inspected the ride carefully. Inspectors found that a wooden support beam had broken under the weight of the heavy train. The dip in the track then jolted the train and the riders. Since then, the record-breaking loop has been removed from Son of Beast. Officials hope to reopen the coaster in 2007, but without the loop. Lighter trains can then be used for a smoother ride.

Like Father, Like Son

Although it is more than 7,000 feet (2,134 m) long, Son of Beast falls short of being the longest wooden roller coaster in the world. That record is held by Son of Beast's "father," The Beast. Both roller coasters are at Paramount King's Island in Cincinnati, Ohio. Built in 1979, The Beast is an amazing 7,359 feet (2,243 m) long. A ride on The Beast lasts for more than four minutes.

Riders reach a top speed of 64 miles (103 km) per hour. They are blasted over two hills, each more than 100 feet (30 m) high. The Beast also has three tunnels and one helix, which is a turn in the track that spins around and around in a spiral like water going down a drain.

ROLLER COASTER

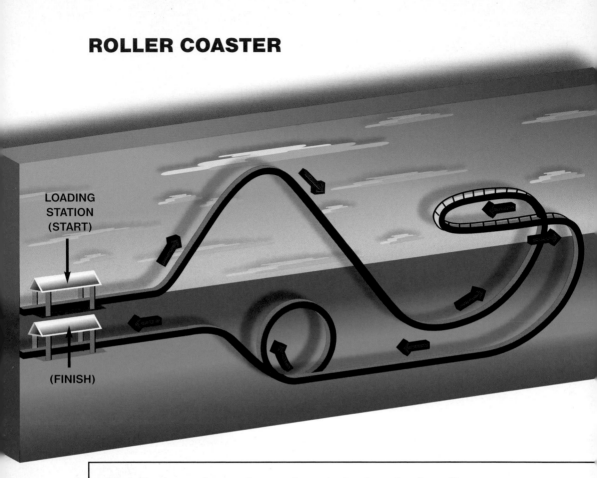

LOADING
STATION
(START)

(FINISH)

The diagram above shows the track of a simple roller coaster.
After a chain or cable pulls the train cars up the first hill, the
coaster relies on natural forces, like gravity and momentum,
to race to the finish. Brakes slow the cars as the ride comes
to an end.

MEGA FACTS

The oldest roller coaster in the United States
is Leap-the-Dips at Lakemont Park in Altoona,
Pennsylvania. It was first opened in 1902 and
still runs today.

CHAPTER 3

HIGHER AND SCARIER THAN EVER

Las Vegas, Nevada, has taken thrill rides to a new extreme. The rides at the Stratosphere Hotel and Casino are no bigger or taller than other thrill rides. What makes them amazing is that they are located near the top of the 1,149-foot- (350-m-) tall Stratosphere Tower that is attached to the hotel! This location makes the Insanity, X-Scream, and Big Shot the highest thrill rides in the world. They combine the excitement of a thrill ride with a natural fear of heights to really pack a punch.

The Stratosphere's rides are on the tower's observation deck. The deck is more than 900 feet (274 m) above the ground. The Big Shot opened with the tower in April 1996. It starts on a platform 921 feet (281 m) in the air. Riders are launched straight up toward the sky at 45 miles (72 km) per hour. They travel on a steel track up the tower's mast to 1,081 feet (329 m) above the ground.

Riders experience 4 *g's*, or four times the force of gravity, as they are shot skyward. As riders begin a freefall back to the platform, they feel the complete weightlessness of negative g's. The trip to the tip of the mast takes only two and a half seconds!

Riders on the X-Scream hover high above
the Las Vegas streets below.

MEGA FACTS

Original plans for the Stratosphere Tower
included a giant gorilla. A 75-foot- (23-m-) tall
mechanical gorilla would carry riders in its hollow
belly up the side of the tower. The gorilla ride
was never built.

Extreme Screams

The X-Scream was the first ride designed for the Stratosphere by roller coaster design company Interactive Rides Inc. It has a 68-foot (21-m) teeter-totter style track on a large steel base. Builders constructed the track and the base of the ride on the ground. Helicopters lifted the sections into place on the tower's deck. It opened on October 31, 2003. Once riders are in their seats, the track is lifted and tilted at the base. A 38-foot- (12-m-) long section of the track actually hangs past the side of the tower's edge after it is lifted. The rider's cars race at 30 miles (48 km) per hour over the edge of the tower to the end of the track.

A Little Insanity

Officials at the Stratosphere were impressed by the X-Scream. They asked the designers at Interactive Rides to design something even better. The result was Insanity the Ride,

High Roller

One of the first rides on top of the Stratosphere was the High Roller. Along with the Big Shot, it opened in April 1996. A basic steel frame roller coaster, the High Roller was the highest roller coaster in the world. It was more than 900 feet (274 m) above the ground.

The High Roller was pretty mild by thrill ride standards. It had 865 feet (264 m) of steel track. Riders rode along the edge of the tower. Although it moved at only 30 miles (48 km) per hour, riders had a scary view of the ground far below them. December 30, 2005, was the last day anyone could ride the High Roller. The people operating the Stratosphere decided to remove it to make room for more exciting rides.

As riders on Insanity the Ride are pulled outward, they have no choice but to look straight down — if they dare!

which opened in March 2005. Insanity is a ride that dangles riders over the edge of the tower in swinglike seats.

A giant arm moves the seats of the ride from the tower deck to open space 64 feet (20 m) past the

MEGA FACTS

Both the X-Scream and Insanity the Ride have broken down and stopped in mid-ride. Power outages and high winds have each been a cause in the failure of the rides. Twice, terrified riders have been left hanging more than 900 feet (274 m) above the ground. Workers helped the riders back onto the tower deck.

edge of the tower. Riders hang more than 900 feet (274 m) above the ground. Powered by electric motors, the ride whirls around at 40 miles (64 km) per hour. As it spins, the seats and riders are pulled outward by centrifugal force.

Riders on the Big Shot make three bungee-cord-like bounces up and down. Each one is a little less gut-wrenching than the first.

CHAPTER 4

SUPER THRILLS

O fficials at Six Flags Magic Mountain in Valencia, California, wanted a roller coaster that would be a one-of-a-kind record breaker. They hired roller coaster design company Intamin AG. Known for creating new and better roller coaster designs, the company came up with Superman the Escape. Opened in March 1997, it is the first roller coaster to break the 100 mile (161 km) per hour mark. At the time, it was also the tallest roller coaster in the world at 415 feet (126 m) high.

As with all steel roller coasters, builders made sections of the 1,235-foot (376-m) track and supporting framework at another location. Once delivered to the coaster site, giant cranes lifted each section into place. Then workers welded them together. That is where the similarities between

MEGA FACTS

Superman the Escape is usually referred to as a shuttle coaster or reverse freefall coaster. True roller coasters have a track where the beginning meets the end in a complete path. A shuttle, or freefall, coaster has two separate ends that never meet.

Virtual Thrills

Modern roller coasters are born in the world of computers. Roller coaster designers have to use science and math to decide how to build the first hill of a coaster. The height and angle of that first hill must provide enough energy to keep the coaster going around the rest of the track. Designers experiment with different twists, turns, and loops without ever building a single thing. The computer model gives the designers a look at how the roller coaster will work.

On Superman the Escape, riders pause for a split second at the top before falling backwards.

MEGA FACTS

Each of the two passenger trains of Superman the Escape weigh more than 6 tons (5 tonnes).

Roller Coasters for Dummies

Roller coaster designers work extra hard to make sure that roller coasters are safe for riders. Once a thrill ride is built, workers run the ride to make sure it works right. Then they place weighted mannequins or sand bags in the train. These "dummies" take the first ride on the coaster to make sure it is safe.

Any problems with the ride are worked out by designers. After the ride is determined to be safe by designers, the workers who built the roller coaster ride on it. Roller coaster inspectors check thrill rides out many times each year. They make sure coasters stay safe for riders. Amusement parks also hire people to inspect the rides each day before they open.

Each dummy on Pennsylvania's Phantom Revenge coaster is filled with **170 pounds (77 kilograms)** of water. Together, they weigh as much as a train full of riders.

Superman the Escape and other steel roller coasters end, however.

Unlike traditional roller coasters, Superman the Escape does not use chains to move its trains. It is able to reach super-hero speeds using motors that have high-powered magnets. The magnets move the roller coaster's train forward along the steel track. They do not hold the train to the track, however. That job is still done by wheels.

Magnets are polarized. One side of a magnet is negative. The other side is positive. When opposite poles touch, the magnets attract each other. They pull themselves together. If the same poles touch, the magnets repel each other. They push each other away. The super-strong magnets on Superman the Escape allow its trains to be launched or stopped. The movement depends on whether the magnets on the track are pushing away or pulling toward the magnets on the trains.

Magnetic Attraction

To board Superman the Escape, passengers walk through a special-effects tunnel full of glowing paint and special lights before they reach the launch area. Once the coaster train is loaded, the high-powered magnets along the L-shaped track react with magnets on the roller coaster train. The magnets launch the train like a slingshot along a 900-foot-(274-m-) long track.

The ride blasts from 0 to 100 miles (161 km) per hour in only seven seconds. Riders experience more than 4 g's as Superman the Escape takes off. Then the magnets on the track and the speed of the train

MEGA FACTS

Astronauts feel a little more than 3 g's when blasting off in the Space Shuttle. That force is less than what riders feel on many extreme roller coasters today.

Wet and Wild

Some thrill rides are real soakers. The tallest water plunge ride in the world is the Perilous Plunge at Knott's Berry Farm in California. The Perilous Plunge is 121 feet (37 m) high. That height is just 34 feet (10 m) shorter than that of Niagara Falls. Riders are hurled along at speeds of up to 50 miles (80 km) per hour as they plummet down a 115-foot (35-m) water chute.

Before the Plunge opened in 2000, the tallest water plunge ride was the Tidal Force in Hershey, Pennsylvania. It opened in May of 1994. The Tidal Force is 100 feet (30 m) high. It reaches a top speed of 53 miles (85 km) per hour.

Water rides like the Perilous Plunge can help cool off riders during a hot day at the amusement park.

combine to shoot it straight up a 41-story, 415-foot (126-m) climb.

After the train reaches the top of the track, it starts to freefall back toward the ground. Riders are still facing skyward and feel six and a half seconds of weightlessness. The magnet system then slows the ride down as riders return to the loading station backward. The entire ride lasts only 26 seconds.

THE ULTIMATE SCREAM MACHINE

On May 21, 2005, Kingda Ka at Six Flags Great Adventure in Jackson, New Jersey, took its place in the record books. It became the tallest and fastest roller coaster in the world. The steel coaster has 3,118 feet (950 m) of steel track. Kingda Ka's top height of 456 feet (139 m) is taller than a 45-story building. It reaches an amazing speed of 128 miles (206 km) per hour. Kingda Ka was designed by Intamin AG. They are the same roller coaster geniuses who designed Superman the Escape.

The King of Coasters

Construction of Kingda Ka began in August 2004. After bulldozers cleared the coaster site, workers dug three 8-foot- (2-m-) deep holes for the tower footings. Each hole was more than 50 feet (15 m) wide. For the rest of the coaster, workers poured 166 concrete footings. It took twenty weeks to complete just the footings.

Construction crews used cranes to lift 40-foot (12-m) steel track sections into place on the tower. Workers bolted the sections together. The track is only 3 feet (1 m) wide. Wind was a huge problem when lifting the steel sections. While the wind might not have blown hard at ground level, it whipped around at 456 feet (139 m) in the air. On very windy days, cranes could

This construction photo shows the topmost section
of Kingda Ka's vertical turn being installed.

not lift the sections into place. The final section was
put into place on January 13, 2005.

Prepare for Takeoff

Like Superman the Escape, Kingda Ka relies on
something other than chains and gravity to get
going. Intamin AG designed the steel giant with the
same type of system that helps launch some military
fighter jets off aircraft carriers.

MEGA FACTS

Japan is home to two of the top five fastest
roller coasters in the world. The Dodonpa steel
coaster can reach 107 miles (172 km) per
hour. The Steel Dragon 2000 travels up to
95 miles (153 km) per hour.

In this giant launching system, two huge motors spin a large rotating drum, winding a thick cable around the drum. The cable is attached to a small "catch car" that runs beneath the tracks. The catch car hooks onto the bottom of the roller coaster train.

The motors spin the drum. The cable and catch car shoot forward, pulling the roller coaster train down the track. When the train reaches top speed, the catch car lets go. Then the ride uses the power of its own momentum to keep going. Amazingly, the whole process of launching the train takes only seven seconds. Several different sets of wheels keep the train from flying off the track. The train has sets of wheels that run on top of, underneath, and on the side of the steel track.

Riders feel 4.5 g's as they take off at 128 miles (206 km) per hour. They blast up a vertical turn of 456 feet (139 m). Riders feel brief weightlessness at the top before they whip straight down

Thrill in a Box

Some thrill seekers never have to leave the comfort of a room. Ridefilms combine the movement of a roller coaster with movie and sound for a whole new experience. The idea behind ridefilms began with flight simulators in the early 1990s. Small rooms were built that looked like the inside of an airplane or Space Shuttle cockpit. The rooms were mounted on machines that would lift and move just like a real aircraft or shuttle. In a ridefilm, people enter a room and buckle themselves into a seat. Once the movie begins, they are hit by movement and sound. The seats feel like they buck, rock, and swoop with the action. In reality, they are only moving a few inches in any direction. Everything is timed so that riders feel as if they are inside the action of the movie.

Safety First

Hurling through the air, hundreds of feet above the ground, faster than a speeding car — these conditions could spell disaster without good safety systems. Roller coasters have to be safe to be fun. Computers have provided the biggest boost in roller coaster safety.

Before computers, people operated a coaster by hand. They controlled its speed and the braking systems. This left a lot of room for human error. Today, computers take the guesswork out of running a coaster. They can be programmed to run the thrill rides with few or no mistakes.

Lap bars (*shown above*) and sometimes shoulder restraints help keep riders safely inside coasters.

through a spiral. The ride reaches more than 100 miles (161 m) per hour again. The train races down a valley and over a final hill.

Magnetic brakes, like those on the X-Scream, pulse to slow the ride down as it reaches the loading station. There is no contact with the brakes and the track. The whole hair-raising ride takes less than a minute. It may not be an F-18 fighter jet or the Space Shuttle, but Kingda Ka is today's ultimate thrill ride!

Thrill seekers on the Kingda Ka prepare for another hair-raising drop.

MEGA FACTS

Before Kingda Ka, the tallest, fastest roller coaster in the world was the Top Thrill Dragster at Cedar Point Theme Park in Sandusky, Ohio. It stands 420 feet (128 m) tall and reaches a top speed of 120 miles (193 km) per hour.

1600s Russian ice slides are built.

1800s Dry slides with rollers are built in France.

1873 Mauch Chunk Switchback Railway becomes the first gravity ride in the United States.

1884 LaMarcus A. Thompson builds the Switchback roller coaster at Coney Island. It is the first roller coaster in the United States.

1895 Sea Lion Park opens at Coney Island. It is the very first amusement park.

1897 Steeplechase Park opens at Coney Island.

1927 The Cyclone roller coaster opens at Coney Island.

1979 The Beast opens at Paramount Kings Island amusement park. At 7,359 feet (2,243 m) long, it is the longest wooden coaster in the world.

1996 The Stratosphere Tower opens with Big Shot and High Roller more than 900 feet (274 m) in the air.

1997 Superman the Escape opens and is the first coaster to break the 100 mile (161 m) per hour mark.

2000 Son of Beast opens and becomes the tallest wooden roller coaster in the world. It is 218 feet (66 m) high.

2005 Kingda Ka opens. It is the tallest and fastest roller coaster in the world. It is 456 feet (139 m) tall and reaches 128 miles (206 km) per hour.

GLOSSARY

attract − to pull to itself or be drawn toward something because of a force or forces

centrifugal force − the force that pulls an object outward when it is rotated, or spun, in a circle

footings − the wide supports at the base of a coaster or other structure that help hold it up

friction − a force that slows motion when two surfaces rub against one another

full-circuit − in thrill rides, a roller coaster whose cars travel around the track in only one direction and end up near the same point where they started

g's − a measurement of the force of gravity. The normal pull of gravity on someone at rest is 1 G.

gravity − the force that pulls things down toward Earth

helix − a spiral shape

momentum − the force that keeps an object moving until it comes to a complete stop

polarized − in magnets, having either a positive or negative end

reinforced concrete − concrete with steel bars or mesh added to it for extra support

repel − to be forced away or apart

simulators − devices or machines that reproduce, or copy, the conditions of a working situation, allowing people to learn and practice tasks safely and inexpensively

terrain − an area of land or the features of its surface, such as hills or valleys

TO FIND OUT MORE

Books

Roller Coaster! Movement and Acceleration. Raintree Fusion: Physical Science (series). Paul Mason (Raintree)

Roller Coaster Science: 50 Wet, Wacky, Wild, Dizzy Experiments About Things Kids Like Best. Jim Wiese (Sagebrush)

Roller Coasters. Crusin' (series). Gil Chandler (Capstone Press)

Roller Coasters. How Are They Built? (series). Lynn M. Stone (Rourke Publishing)

Video

Modern Marvels: Rollercoasters: Search for the Ultimate Thrill (The History Channel) NR

Thrill Ride − The Science of Fun (Sony Pictures) G

Web Sites

Design A Roller Coaster

www.learner.org/exhibits/parkphysics/coaster

Build a roller coaster and see if it is both thrilling and safe.

Roller Coasters

www.ultimaterollercoaster.com

Read more about roller coasters and thrill rides.

Publisher's note to educators and parents: Our editors have carefully reviewed these Web sites to ensure that they are suitable for children. Many Web sites change frequently, however, and we cannot guarantee that a site's future contents will continue to meet our high standards of quality and educational value. Be advised that children should be closely supervised whenever they access the Internet.

INDEX

About the Author

Susan K. Mitchell never met a roller coaster she would not ride. She is a teacher and author of several children's picture books. Susan has also written many non-fiction chapter books for kids. She lives near Houston, Texas, with her husband, two daughters, a dog, and two cats. She dedicates this book to her dad, William, who loves roller coasters as much as she does.